I0829751

The Shit Zone

Welcome to Your Changed Self

Thoraiya Kanafani, PhD

authorHOUSE®

AuthorHouse™ UK
1663 Liberty Drive
Bloomington, IN 47403 USA
www.authorhouse.co.uk
Phone: 0800.197.4150

© 2019 Thoraiya Kanafani, PhD. All rights reserved.

No part of this book may be reproduced, stored in a retrieval system, or transmitted by any means without the written permission of the author.

Published by AuthorHouse 01/15/2019

ISBN: 978-1-7283-8356-9 (sc)
ISBN: 978-1-7283-8357-6 (hc)
ISBN: 978-1-7283-8355-2 (e)

Print information available on the last page.

Any people depicted in stock imagery provided by Getty Images are models, and such images are being used for illustrative purposes only.
Certain stock imagery © Getty Images.

This book is printed on acid-free paper.

Because of the dynamic nature of the Internet, any web addresses or links contained in this book may have changed since publication and may no longer be valid. The views expressed in this work are solely those of the author and do not necessarily reflect the views of the publisher, and the publisher hereby disclaims any responsibility for them.

CONTENTS

ACKNOWLEDGMENTS

This book was inspired by all the people who have had the courage and the strength to venture out of their comfort zone, ultimately their Shit Zone, and into their Happy Zone.

I am grateful to all of my friends, colleagues, students, interns, and clients for inspiring me to write this book. I would like to thank Nadia for helping me complete this book without searching for a ditch in which to bury both my manuscript and myself. I'd also like to thank people who share names with those I used for this book, who involuntarily volunteered their names as culturally vague. However, above all, I would have to say that I am mostly grateful to my family for their presence in my life and their influence on its progression.

PREFACE

One of the reasons why I decided to write this book is that I fucking hate pop psychology. I can't stand how people have been pushing this agenda of so-called "happiness" and the idea that everybody needs to be happy, content, satisfied, and over the top. Let's sell happiness this way, let's get happy that way, and let's all combine our happiness and fucking be happy together. Yuck and gag! This book is about realizing the reality of happiness, which is that it doesn't fucking exist in the way pop psychology is marketing it. I'm not saying happiness doesn't exist at all, but the way people are selling it is bullshit and needs to be called out as such.

So the reason why I don't describe what happiness and the Happy Zone are in this book is because I don't know what makes you happy, I'm not *going* to know what makes you happy, and you probably don't fucking know what makes you happy right now anyway. I'm not going to claim to know anything about your happiness because we are all different and happiness means something different to each of us, but through your own exploration, self-awareness, and insight into your life, you'll come to realize what your happiness means and what makes you happy. You'll figure out what moves you out of your Shit Zone and into a zone in which you feel more content. You'll stop feeling like "My life is shit, and every day feels like shit."

Another reason why I decided to write this book is that one of the things that I consistently find amongst most of my clients and many people I know is that they are fighting—on a day-to-day, week-to-week basis—through their shit. They suffer through everything I mention in this book, yet they keep fighting. A lot of people don't understand how that fight, in and of itself, can lead to that quick resignation: "Fuck it, I don't want to do this anymore." But a lot of people keep fighting, and if I absolutely have to refer to something millennial, it is that the struggle is fucking real. Making that shift from a Shit Zone to a Happy Zone takes not only a lot of strength and courage, but also resilience, continuity, and consistency. I have a lot of admiration and pride in seeing my clients and people whom I know push through their shit, so I decided to honor them with a book that I hope they can connect to.

A lot of people ask me how I can do this work without getting depressed by all the stories I hear.

Something that comes to me really quickly is that yes, I deal with a lot of sadness, shit, and unhappiness, but also with a lot of triumph, perseverance, and resilience. As cheesy as this might sound, it's the latter part that motivates me to continue my work. Triumph, perseverance, and resilience, I believe, are far more important than any kind of success or failure in life. Because ultimately when you talk about success and failure, you're really just forcing yourself to look at life with a binary focus. Things are always either this or that: I either succeeded or failed; I did either good or bad. But life is not black and white; it's gray, and there are many shades of gray in life (no pun intended).

It's not supposed to be that simple, unfortunately. Life is a mess.

Life is complicated, complex, chaotic, fucked, stupid, and so many other negative things. And yet, despite all of that, it's also fucking amazing. Only when you see life for all its intensity and amazingness can you truly progress and move past the shit that you have continuously dealt with in this life.

I called this book *The Shit Zone* because every time I'm with a client, they tell me they feel like shit. So instead of calling it the comfort zone, which it's not because nobody is fucking comfortable in it, it's the Shit Zone. It's exactly that because they feel like shit.

Throughout the book, I mention the Shit Zone Brain, which is basically your brain in the Shit Zone. What that means is that your brain convinces you that you're safer there. It's the brain that keeps you in the Shit Zone, because it has built all the mechanisms it needs to protect you in its own fucked-up way. But once you start to make strides to get out of the Shit Zone, your brain changes and, by doing so, your life is transformed into something that's a little less shitty.

I don't mention the Happy Zone Brain because I don't know what your Happy Zone is, so I don't know what your brain is going to look like in your Happy Zone. That's something for you to figure out. However, I can tell you that your Happy Zone Brain will consistently evolve and will not stagnate at any point in your life, even if the changes are minute.

Change does not have to be some monumental shift; it can occur in the smallest of ways. Take this quotation by James Watkins, American journalist and television news anchor: "A river cuts through rock, not because of its power, but because of its persistence." The water applies small amounts of pressure against the rocks for long periods of time before the rock breaks. Don't think that making small changes and keeping at it isn't worth it. Sometimes they are the incentives that help us make the big changes. They teach us to look a little deeper, test the water, and adjust our strategies. Making small changes may help get you closer to where you want to go, but persistence makes it worth it.

BEFORE WE START

Take a few minutes and think about your life. Where are you in terms of your goals and vision? What goals do you want to achieve in your life?

Now name three things that you would like to change in your current life in order to achieve those goals. Be specific. We will explore them again at the end of this book.

INTRODUCTION

The only thing that is constant is change.

—Heraclitus

This is not a self-help book. It's not even a how-to book. Let's call it a wake-up call. You may gain everything, a few things, or nothing from reading it. The process is yours to explore and make your own.

What is it about change? What makes it so intimidating and worthy of resistance? What keeps us in the same shit, despite our conscious acknowledgment of the need to get the hell out of it?

Change has such power, such rigor, and it can be such a debilitating prison. Whatever it is goes beyond sense or logic. On a collective level, we are not very resistant to change. Evolutionarily, we've naturally changed and adapted to our environment in response to difficulties we've experienced. Physical and genetic changes have occurred since our species first existed. For example, our bodies are generally lighter, smaller boned, and shorter, and our brains have shrunk by 100 to 150 cubic centimeters less than when we first appeared. The list goes on. However, on an individual level, we struggle to change and adapt, which makes it difficult for us to overcome what keeps us in our shit.

For years, I have watched my clients struggle with change and resist walking a different path. Over time, experience, and then implementation, the reasons for resisting the shift from their Shit Zone to their Happy Zone become apparent and involve many variables.

Let's explore these variables before examining the path. The Shit Zone is equivalent to your comfort zone, but it does not coincide with feelings of comfort. Consider this to be a way of life that includes all the aspects that are understood and clear, yet do not promote satisfaction or happiness. Rather, it is a state of being in which the safety of your discomfort you are in outweighs the possibility of being happy.

The reason why the term *'shit'* is used as the adjective to describe the zone is that most of my clients describe it as "feeling like shit" whilst in this zone. I can imagine the feelings associated with the zone would be synonymous with sitting in a pile of shit without the smell: warm, cozy, and familiar, and yet you want to get out as fast as possible. And if we think back to infancy for a second, we weren't happy to sit in shit then, so why are we now?

THE COMFORT OF IT ALL LEADS TO SHITTY FEELINGS

The next variable is the Happy Zone, which is self-explanatory and applies to the individual, not the collective. However, this is not a zone where discomfort does not reside. Instead, it's the zone where discomfort is accepted and does not significantly affect the status quo of a person's feelings. It is NOT the absence of shit, but rather the understanding of how to cope with and overcome shit when it shows up. Every single person has an idea of what their Happy Zone looks like, even if it's just "not where I am now." However, this idea at times is so abstract that it makes the notion of attaining it seem overwhelmingly bleak. The Happy Zone is where someone wants to be.

Unfortunately, the idea of being happy has become a trend. People strive for happiness before they even know how to define it. Self-help books (ironic, I know), workshops, trainings, self-exploration, and actualization classes all aimed to encourage people to be happy and achieve a state of happiness. What horrible pressure to put on people! How someone can justify pressuring others to be in a state that they deem happy is beyond egotistical. What gives anyone the right to do so—and how can they possibly know what makes you happy? How is it that they know more about what makes you "happy"? Well, the answer is that they can't! Their intention is pure enough: they want you to feel happy and satisfied with your life. But just because something works for them doesn't mean it will work for you. So instead of trying to implement others' ideas and concepts of happiness, find your own. The expectations that social media, marketing companies, and society have forced on us in terms of how to define happiness is unrealistic for many people. They imply that we have control over everything in life and can control our own happiness by doing things. The idea of achieving happiness—a construct that is so malleable at every moment of life—is similar to juggling Jell-O.

What makes us happy one day may not necessarily coincide with what make us happy the next week or month or year. Society's idea of being happy implies the notion that we need to be joyous of our lives on a moment to moment basis, which is close to impossible; what is possible, however, is the idea that we can find peace in the ups and downs of our lives, regardless of what comes along. Imagine the pressure that people place on themselves to be happy with everything in their lives. Even though that may not be what the promoters of happiness intend, their audience of such mass marketing mistakenly understands it as such.

One of the greatest symbols of coexistence, in my opinion, is the yin-yang symbol, which highlights the balance of life. To achieve balance, opposites must coexist and possess parts of each other within their own existences. The yin-yang symbol dates back to ancient China, and the patterns and relationships that occurred in nature were greatly studied by the Chinese. They found that everything in life existed in relation to its surrounding environment and would need a counterpart in order to live in harmony. The yin-yang symbol came to signify that everything in existence consists of two forces that are both complementary and oppositional.

Yin and yang refers to the fact that all things occur in pairs and that those same things could have both properties of one another. Yin is depicted by the black side of the symbol, and yang is the white side. The representation of the philosophy of yin and yang, also known as the Tai Chi symbol, lies in both the individual aspects and the entirety of yin and yang. The outer circle symbolizes the duality of everything that exists in the universe; the black yin section represents characteristics such as female, intuitive, creative, dark, and soft, etc.; and the white yang section represents characteristics such as male, logical, bright, strong, light, and so on.

The two sections signify the interactive and cyclical nature of everything. The smaller circles demonstrate that nothing is absolute and that in each portion, there is a small bit of the other portion. Nothing in the universe is either black or white; everything contains a bit of each, necessarily existing in each other. The S-shape that divides the yin and yang is indicative of the flow between them. As one side swells in size, the other shrinks to accommodate for it, but neither ever disappears.

This corresponds to the idea of happiness; true happiness exists only in the presence of sadness, though it can exist within sadness as well. This concept will be explained further in chapter 2.

The final but most crucial variable in this book is the process of shifting from the Shit Zone to the Happy Zone, which holds the key to a successful one-way shift. This process of the shift involves an array of subvariables that contribute to resistance, continuation, and extinction, as well as acceptance of the transition itself. The subvariables, which include sadness, fear, worry, guilt, and regret, will be discussed further in chapter 4.

To conclude this book, questions will be posed as a way to help people transition from one zone to another.

By no means is this process finite. The shift from Shit Zone to Happy Zone can be recreated over and over again if your new Happy Zone becomes your next Shit Zone. This will all become clearer as you read through the book.

LET'S TALK ABOUT YOUR SHIT

Describe where you are right now in your life. What's wrong with it? What in your life is not making you happy? What do you feel is missing? How does it feel to be in this particular place in your life?

CHAPTER 1

Variable 1: The Shit Zone

Take a minute and think about where you are in your life. Don't think of what you have or don't have in terms of possessions. Rather, consider what you value in life and whether you are working toward satisfying those values. Think of values as principles or standards that are important to you. You use these standards to motivate and guide yourself through life. If you feel as though it is something you must do, it's not a value.

Examples of values include self-care, honesty, intimacy, commitment, responsibility, respect, trust, and authenticity. No one behaves perfectly according to the values they deem important. There's always a margin of error. For instance, you may value honesty in yourself and others, but no one is honest 100 percent of the time. On average, we lie about five to seven times a day, so it's not likely that we'll be honest all the time. Therefore, we give ourselves a little leeway when we talk about behaving according to our values.

Nevertheless, identifying your values and behaving in view of them keeps you out of your Shit Zone.

To make sure you are behaving according to your values, you have to ask yourself, "Am I living my values?" For instance, if you value relationships in your life, are you behaving in ways that can strengthen the chances of developing meaningful ones? If you consider this question and find that you're not actually living your values, you're in a Shit Zone. Remember that you don't have to behave according to your value system in a perfect way or even at every point in your life. But if you are not working toward your values, then welcome to your Shit Zone.

Your Shit Zone, as mentioned in the introduction, is essentially your comfort zone with one major difference: you're not very emotionally comfortable in it. You might find solace and satisfaction in the fact that the variables and routine of your life are well known to you, but deep down, you are missing key elements that block your emotional comfort and satisfaction.

Let us imagine that for a second you're in a job that brings you no satisfaction at all; but hey, it pays the bills, however, so your Shit Zone brain tells you that the financial trade-off is above and beyond any necessity for personal job satisfaction. Pshh. Job satisfaction is a new-aged illusion. Say hello to the rationalization of your Shit Zone brain, which is telling you that if you look beyond where you are right now, you don't know what will happen, so why risk it? Let's just stay where we are, because life is safer in here. What your Shit Zone brain does not want you to know is that life is not in black and white; you don't have to leave your job to have job satisfaction.

You could consider other options. For example, you could look for roles and responsibilities within the company that spark your interest and thus improve your job satisfaction in a different way. You could take on a second, part-time job to satisfy your passion, or you could take up a hobby as a way to make up for the possible misery you may feel in your job. But no, you stay in your Shit Zone because your Shit Zone brain convinces you that it is your only option because the alternative could be worse.

Perhaps it would be a good idea to examine the defense mechanisms used by the Shit Zone brain that assist us in keeping ourselves in our Shit Zone. At times, defense mechanisms can help us deal with emotions that we are not ready or willing to process. For instance, a person who experiences a trauma might benefit from repressing the associated emotions until they are prepared emotionally and psychologically to do so. Therefore, defense mechanisms can work to our advantage and be helpful in many scenarios. At other times, however, defense mechanisms are used in a negative way. Although we might benefit from seeing reality, they blind us to it because of the distress it could cause us.

Before delving into the different types of defense mechanisms, let's take a look at the definition of trauma. Trauma must be looked at in two different but connected ways: as an exposure to a stressful or disturbing event, and as the emotional and psychological response to that event. Now here's where it gets a bit tricky: the subjective definition of trauma. Because of how they define trauma, many people who talk about their traumatic experiences will minimize them. Either (1) their experiences don't seem significant when they compare them with other people's trauma, (2) other people have minimized what they experienced, or (3) they don't want to think of themselves as having experienced trauma.

Stop for a second, and read those options again.

First, comparing your trauma with other people's trauma? This would have to be, by far, one of the most horrendous ways to invalidate your experiences. "I haven't been sexually assaulted or been through war, so how could I say what I experienced was a trauma?" Insert shocked-face emoji here, please. Basically, that thought process implies that only people who have been sexually assaulted or experienced war have the right or deserve to say that they have been traumatized. Therefore, abusive treatment by parents, friends, or partner; childhood abandonment; death of loved ones; medical illness revelations; bullying; identity theft; harsh breakups; car accidents (either observed or experienced); gaslighting; financial bankruptcy; and so many more experiences are just routine events that cause no psychological or emotional disturbances or distress. Bullshit!

Second, because other people have minimized what you experienced? This is something people all over the world experience, but it is perhaps most prevalent in the Asian subcontinent, Middle Eastern, and African regions:

- Sexual abuse of children by a family member or friend? "It happens to everyone. It's not such a big deal. Get over it."

- Physical abuse of children? "That's how I was raised, and I turned out fine."

- Physical or emotional marital abuse? "Maybe you made them angry. You can't just leave your family; you owe it to them to stay."

- Heartbreak? "It's your own fault."

- Mental health difficulties? "You're just sensitive. Go take a walk, and you'll be fine."

- Learning disorders? "You're just lazy. You don't study hard enough."

The feelings of shame and embarrassment are avoided and denied (to be discussed later) to a level where invalidation and minimization are used to maintain a status quo of comfort.

And third, because you don't want to think of yourself as someone who has experienced trauma? What does that even mean? Is the assumption that, as humans, we don't experience trauma at all? Unless you live in a bubble and are surrounded by roses and kittens all day (which, ironically, would be traumatic to some), you have experienced a trauma in your life, whether you want to admit it or not. However, that doesn't mean that you have not been able to work through your trauma and continue on with your life. Admitting that you have experienced trauma doesn't mean that you have post-traumatic stress disorder

(PTSD); this is probably where the confusion lies. Experiencing trauma in your life is just part of being human and living in general.

Suffering from PTSD is quite different in that it involves an amalgamation of symptomology, such as exposure to actual or threatened death, serious injury, or sexual violence. These can be direct experiences or a person can witness such a traumatic event, learn of it happening to someone close, or experience repeated exposure to aversive details of the traumatic event. This symptom is accompanied by the presence of intrusion symptoms (flashbacks, distressing dreams, physiological reactions, and so on), persistent avoidance of stimuli, negative changes in cognitions and mood (paranoia), and/or changes in arousal and reactivity (all trauma associated) that last more than a month and cause significant disturbance to a person's social, academic, or occupational functioning. As you can see, PTSD is a lot more complicated than trauma.

Defense mechanisms are strategies that we use to protect ourselves from anxiety or guilt provoked by unacceptable thoughts or feelings. These strategies are psychological safety nets that we implement unconsciously and not always in negative ways.

Rationalization

Rationalization, as mentioned before, is by far one of the most widely used defense mechanisms. As described by Anna Freud, Sigmund Freud's daughter (yep, that Freud), it is the cognitive distortion of reality to make the event or impulse less threatening (Freud, 1937). Plainly put, it is our way to justify why we did or said what we did. For example, if you yell at another person, you're likely to rationalize why you did so by saying the other person pissed you off rather than take the emotional hit that you didn't control your emotional outburst in that moment.

Many couples love this defense mechanism. They rationalize why they react in negative ways by justifying their reactions were in response to their partner's action. For every action, there is an equal and opposite reaction, right? Wrong! The fact that you yelled at your husband or wife because he or she made you angry is not justifiable or rational. It is an excuse you give yourself for losing your shit and not emotionally self-regulating so you can sleep better at night. This is not blame; this is awareness that even though it might feel better to rationalize your anger that way, it's not accurate. You don't yell at your boss at work when he or she makes you angry. That means you are capable of regulating your emotions when someone provokes you. Yet you do not do it with your loved one.

Let's examine some other defense mechanisms first proposed by Sigmund Freud.

Repression

Repression is an unconscious strategy that keeps painful thoughts and feelings hidden and inaccessible to the conscious mind. For instance, in a traumatic experience, the survivor's unconscious might repress memories and details of the event to avoid further emotional, psychological, and physiological pain and turmoil.

For example, as a child, Joanna witnessed her father physically abusing her mother for many years. She repressed this memory and did not understand why she was so scared of developing relationships with men when they got angry. In her previous relationships, she froze when her boyfriends confronted her in any way. She avoided confrontation and disagreement at all costs by submitting to anything they wanted. She felt consistently nervous and fearful in her relationships, until she realized that she had been repressing memories of her father's abusive treatment of her mother. Now that she has processed those memories successfully, Joanna is able to discuss her concerns with her new boyfriend while asserting her feelings and thoughts in the relationship in an effective manner without fearing his possible reaction.

Projection

This is probably the defense mechanism most often used by people against one another in arguments. "It's not *me*, it's *you*" is the strategy of assigning to other people your own thoughts, feelings, and behaviors. People with social anxiety do this quite often when their own self-perception and fear they have of social situations becomes what they think people are thinking, feeling, or behaving. For example, if you judge yourself to be boring, you might believe that other people find you boring as well, even if you're actually the life of the gathering, or perhaps you might think that other people are boring.

One of the many ways that projection can rear its ugly head is in sibling arguments. For example, Nadia and Diana, three years apart, are the only children in the family. Naturally, they argue, as all siblings do. However, Diana is self-absorbed, obsessive, competitive, vengeful, and continuously holds grudges when it suits her. She does not consider perspectives other than her own, and she will argue down a point until there's nothing left. On the other hand, Nadia is a people pleaser with underdeveloped cajónes. When Diana and Nadia argue, Diana calls Nadia a selfish, egotistical, neurotic, and bitter bitch. In doing so, she is projecting her feelings about her inadequacy onto Nadia to protect herself from recognizing the fact that she actually possesses those characteristics.

Denial

Denial occurs when a person perceives the reality of their situation as too much to handle and responds by blocking it from awareness. Imagine witnessing a child on a bike being hit by a car. That event is too much for anyone to handle, so you block it from your awareness and deny that you saw it. Another example that might strike closer to home is your reaction to the death of a loved one. Your initial response might be denial, as a way to avoid believing the reality of such a significant loss.

Let's talk about Sam. Sam is a middle-aged man who still lives at home with his mother and father. He is the only child of traditional parents who have never accepted any disobedience or rebellion from him. Sam insists that his parents are loving and caring, despite his inability to describe any instance when he felt love or caring from either of them. He has struggled to find a partner, get a job, and move out of his parents' house, yet he attributed all of his shortcomings to his own failure. Sam strongly refuses to assign any responsibility to his parents even though ever since he could remember, his mother and father used to criticize him and consistently tell him what a failure he would turn out to be. Sam is in denial, refusing to believe the reality of his situation out of fear that he will be alone if he does so.

Displacement

Displacement is the defense mechanism that involves satisfying an impulse or motive with a substitute. For instance, if your superiors make your life hell at work, instead of taking your anger out on them and getting fired, when you get home you yell at your spouse, kids, goldfish, and so on.

Let's examine Grace's situation. Grace is studying philosophy at the university. During her stint, she prefers partying with her friends most nights rather than studying for her midterms and finals. So obviously, when she doesn't get the final grades that she wants, she doesn't take responsibility for her misplaced priorities. Instead, she displaces blame onto her professors for not writing a fair exam and onto her friends for distracting her and "forcing" her to go out rather than staying home and studying.

Regression

Regression, by far my favorite one, is the defense strategy of going back in psychological time to when you were younger when faced with stressful situations. A person might even assume the fetal position when feeling sad or vulnerable (classic duvet/personal/ mental health day behavior).

Maria worked at a hospital as a pediatric surgeon. She is a single mom of two kids and under a tremendous amount of stress. During their regular squabbles, Maria acts more like a child than her teenage daughter. Maria literally stomps her feet and scoffs when she becomes angry and frustrated, instead of engaging in a mature conversation. Instead, Maria's stressful life and reactions regress her behavior to that of a five-year-old throwing a tantrum.

Sublimation

Another defense mechanism is sublimation, which involves dealing with a socially unacceptable impulse, such as aggression, in a socially acceptable way, like boxing.

Mike loves food so much that he became a chef. As a child, he was on the chubby side and never left any food on his plate. He often overate and would not only finish the food on his plate, but ate his family members' leftovers. Teased and mocked for being heavier than the other kids, he started taking care of himself and eating moderately until he had lost quite a bit of weight. However, his internal impulse to overeat was never satisfied, so he became a chef as a way to control and transform that impulse into something more socially acceptable.

Reaction Formation

This defense mechanism is reaction formation, which happens when a person acts in direct opposition to how they feel. For example, imagine someone who hates their teacher, but instead of showing that, they go out of their way to be nice to the teacher and do well in class.

Kaya and Omar have been best friends for a long time and hold similar opinions about most things. Omar enjoys using S&M practices (pain for pleasure) during sexual experiences, but he hasn't told Kaya, because she has voiced a negative opinion about people who engage in S&M play. Consequently, Omar hides his true feelings and urges by joining Kaya at judging and condemning people who participate in such acts. Because of his fear of her reaction, Omar hides his true feelings and displays reaction formation to his urges.

Intellectualization

The final defense mechanism we'll discuss is intellectualization. There are more but for the sake of not overloading you, let's focus on these main ones. It's usually associated with, but is different from, rationalization. Intellectualization is used to avoid feeling any kind of emotional distress. This involves a thoughtful analysis of an event without much regard to how you felt during the situation itself.

Chris' father died of cancer six months ago. Chris had been experiencing difficulty breathing, night sweats, clammy hands, and difficulty concentrating.

After visiting a physician, he was referred to a psychologist to rule out an anxiety disorder. During the visit, Chris described his father's passing in the following ways: the manner in which he died, how long it took, planning the eventual funeral, taking care of his mother and siblings afterwards, and the financial stress it added to his life. In the subsequent sessions, the psychologist noted that Chris did not express and diverted attention away from his feelings regarding his father's death. Chris was intellectualizing.

So how do these defense mechanisms rear their heads in relation to the Shit Zone Brain? Well, let's go through that. First we need a scenario, so let's revisit the job satisfaction story line.

- Rationalization: I stay in this job because it's financially advantageous to do so.

- Repression: It's tough, but I actually feel good in this job. (You're ignoring the fact that your mental health has deteriorated since you took the job.)

- Denial: My job is great and I have no real problems in it. (You're ignoring the fact that you're yelled at and demeaned daily.)

- Projection: My boss hates me and doesn't think I deserve this job. (The truth is that you don't like your boss and don't think you deserve your job.)

- Displacement: Since I can't yell at my boss, I'll just yell at everyone else. (Unconscious thought, of course.)

- Regression: My colleague asked me to cover her shift because of a family emergency. But since I don't like this job, I'm going to say no, even though I could easily do it with no interruption or negative repercussions for me. When I tell her, I might even huff and puff at her and then storm off. (That's what a child would do.)

- Sublimation: I dislike my job and everyone at my office treats me horribly, which makes me very angry. However, since I cannot yell at and be rude to them, I'll go to the gym after work and release my frustration by beating the shit out of the punching bag.

- Intellectualization: I have problems at work but it's fine; it doesn't bother me.

By using any of these defense mechanisms, you're able to stay in your job, even though it makes you unhappy and doesn't fulfill you in any way. So your

Shit Zone Brain persuades you to stay in your Shit Zone by tricking you into believing that it's the best thing for you.

Now that you've seen these defense mechanisms applied practically to real-life situations, you can better understand how they can be easily used to keep you in your Shit Zone. These strategies are mostly unconscious, but they're powerful enough to convince you that what you're doing, or rather not doing, is the best thing for you. The fact that you are not truly emotionally, psychologically, or mentally satisfied in your Shit Zone is not something of which you are overly aware. Rather, defense mechanisms keep you clouded from the true reality in which you live. You continue to live in a safe, comfortable space known as the Shit Zone. Although it has its function of safety, it minimizes the likelihood that you'll ever achieve what you set out to achieve. Remember, stay away from extremes…even defense mechanisms have their advantages at times.

The Shit Zone Brain contributes to feelings of helplessness, hopelessness, loneliness, and/ or eventual indifference, which are contributors to depression and anxiety. By encouraging you – through coercion – into staying in your Shit Zone, feelings of unhappiness and dissatisfaction build up in your life. You feel helpless, causing you to feel like you are unable to control your situation and that you can't really do much about your environment, which leads you to believe that nothing will ever change and that your future is bleak and gloomy.

The feeling of loneliness stems from the thought that you're alone in this experience and nobody else can understand it. You think, *Everyone else has it together, and no one has ever experienced this before.* Finally, indifference occurs when you give up on your situation because of helplessness, hopelessness, and loneliness, and unfortunately, you eventually give up on yourself. Your Shit Zone Brain has almost guaranteed the likelihood that you'll stay in your Shit Zone.

Check Your Shit

This first chapter was a bit heavy, so before we move on, I want to check in and see how you are feeling and maybe allow you to reflect on some of the things that were discussed. Trauma, for example. *Your* trauma, not your compared-against-others trauma. Write a list of the experiences you've had in your life that have negatively affected you in one way or another. You may not even know which experiences have affected you, so start with all negative experiences and then look into how you think they could have affected you.

Defense mechanisms: Were you able to recognize which ones you use and when? It might be a good idea to jot those down here so you can remember them the next time they come up. Awareness is the key to change, and without it, you won't know what you need to change. So write down a few of the defense mechanisms you have used in the past and use specific examples of when you used them.

Let's Get Cheesy, But in a Realistic Way

23

What are the things that would make you happy? Do not include possessions or superficial gratifications! Think of the things you value in life, and try to think of the ones that are missing.

CHAPTER 2

Variable 2: The Happy Zone

In no way should you consider this zone to be the euphoric, ideal reality that is being sold to people. Basically, it's not even close to the new-age happiness bubble that is being marketed to the public. In this book, *Happy Zone* refers to a mental space in which you have satisfied your own self in ways which allow you to embody, in the most realistic sense, your values, priorities, and self-care.

Simply put, the Happy Zone is where you are if you're not in the Shit Zone; exploring what's in the Happy Zone is an impossible feat without the details of the Shit Zone. Remember the yin-yang philosophy? Well, this is based on that. You can't know what makes you happy until you know what makes you unhappy, and vice versa. The assumption that one size fits all or that there's a cookie-cutter definition of the Happy Zone is incorrect. Each person, depending on their own circumstances, must find what their Happy Zone looks like and what works best for them to get there. The vagueness of the description and the process of getting there is frustrating, so let's explore it through examples. First, however, we need to highlight important facets of the Happy Zone.

Acceptance is by far the most important aspect of the Happy Zone. It's not easy for people to accept the fact that the Happy Zone does not include any sort of perfection, nor will it ever. Usually when someone works really hard to get themselves out of their Shit Zone—and make no mistake, it's a difficult process—the expectation is that at the other end of the tunnel, they'll find bliss and peace. That is a dangerous assumption and goal, since that's not always the case.

Let's examine acceptance in a way that is familiar to people who suffer with social anxiety. People who experience social anxiety worry constantly about what others think about them, so they work hard to establish and maintain an image that satisfies those people in the hope that they will escape judgment. One of the problems, however, is that the person with social anxiety has to continuously change who they are, what they like, and how they project that image and behavior based on who they are with at any given time. That shifting sense of self-identity leads to confusion of their self-worth and contributes to a shaky sense of self. Another problem is that the degree to which a person fears judgment from others is generally equivalent to the degree to which others are judging them anyway. No matter what you do, or say, people will always judge you.

We are all human, are we not? It is perfectly natural for us to judge other people, no matter how much we try not to. Our judgments might not come from a negative standpoint, but they are judgments nonetheless. As humans, our brains categorize everything and create what psychologists call schemas, or mental representations, of everything that we know so that we can recall and retrieve information more quickly. Judging something to be good/bad, right/wrong, stupid/weird, and so on is our way of making sense of what we are experiencing. Judgments are a natural part of being human—so yes, everyone judges everyone, whether they admit it or not.

The fear of being judged also ties in to the fear of not being liked. Now let's make one fact perfectly clear before we continue: not everyone likes you. Yes, you! You, him, her, them, everyone! Nor will that ever happen. There's always going to be someone who doesn't like you. Even the most likeable people in Hollywood have haters, and so do you. For example, if you have five friends with whom you routinely hang out, three of them find you funny and enjoy your sense of humor, but the other two do not. If you change to appease the other two, then the three who liked you previously won't appreciate your new humor. Get the point? You'll never please everyone. Therefore, someone is bound not to like you.

Now let's consider acceptance. When people who suffer from social anxiety accept these facts, they learn to be less anxious in social situations. They also learn to develop an acceptance for their own qualities, both good and bad. That acceptance will attract positive relationships and weed out the toxic ones. Acceptance of your own qualities and, entire being, renders other people's opinions of you pointless. Don't misunderstand what is being said here! This is not carte blanche to be a selfish, self-centered asshole. This is a wake-up call to self-reflection. You need to be honest with yourself. Once that's done, you see which qualities match your values and which don't, and then you work to make adjustments. For example, if you identify that you are both stubborn and controlling, you might decide that stubbornness doesn't contradict your values but being controlling does, so you work to become less controlling. Then you become more accepting of the fact that you are stubborn and still slightly controlling. Let's remember that qualities are on a continuum, and it's not that we're either this or that. We slide along the continuum of being too much of this and much less of that.

Back to acceptance and the Happy Zone. That long rant is to highlight that acceptance of the reality of life. Life isn't going to be perfect or the way you want it to be. Some things aren't going to work out and you're going to continue to have hardship, because your happy zone is not a perfect zone. But when you accept that reality of life, the good and the bad, your happy zone becomes more attainable.

Direct your attention back to the idea of yin and yang. In every Happy Zone, there will be moments of sadness, anger, and frustration, and even moments resembling the previously exiled Shit Zone. The very idea of this zone does not live in perfection, but in the acceptance that perfection does not exist and that more good than bad is the goal. If acceptance of this reality is denied or rejected, the likelihood that a Happy Zone will be achieved is slim to none or at the very least, once entered, will be short-lived.

Another feature of the Happy Zone that must be acknowledged is that it constantly changes and cannot be stagnantly lived in forever. It takes work, like any relationship; and this is *your* relationship with *you*. As you change daily, so do your wishes and desires change as well, thus altering your Happy Zone. This does not mean that your Happy Zone will change into another Shit Zone, which you will have to work hard to exit. It just means that you'll have to reevaluate your Happy Zone every once in a while to ensure that you are still where you want to be, and that you're still satisfying the very reasons that originally motivated you to shift into your Happy Zone to begin with.

This is actually a great aspect of the Happy Zone, because the things we may value at twenty years old will not be the same as the things we value at forty. Therefore, it is to our advantage that our values, desires, and aspirations continue to evolve as we do. Furthermore, this constant change allows us to grow and progress as individuals, rather than live in a state of inactivity.

The following are the stories of three people who shifted to their Happy Zones:

Sarah

Sarah was a people pleaser. She always did what she thought everyone around her wanted from her. She didn't speak her mind or voice her opinion, because she worried about being judged or rejected. Despite being a successful business owner, dedicated mother, and devoted wife, Sarah felt an emptiness in her life. She thought that everyone's love and care for her was conditional on whether or not she granted their requests, and she didn't want to risk losing people in her life by asking for what she wanted.

Sarah had always dreamed of writing a children's book series that she had created when she was ten years old. She had even sketched out, from her imagination, what the characters looked like, and she dreamed of eventually turning her books into a movie or TV series. However, when Sarah was in her teens, her teachers and parents had discouraged her from pursuing what they called her "pipe dream," claiming that it wouldn't generate enough income to support her and her future family. They told her that dreams only come true for one-percenters. Sarah was unfulfilled and unhappy in her life, but she didn't feel like anything could or would change.

With no regard for her emotional well-being, Sarah's Shit Zone Brain convinced her that her dream was futile and that she should stick to living in her Shit Zone because she was safe there. She rationalized, denied, and used other unconscious defense mechanisms to keep herself in the Shit Zone that she was used to. However, her Happy Zone was where she really wanted to be, and after some work, it began to solidify.

However, Sarah had to accept the fact that life in her Happy Zone wasn't perfect. Although she found time to write her books, they were not accepted for publication, so she had to publish them herself. Obviously that also indicated that they probably would never become a movie or TV series. Nevertheless, by accepting that her Happy Zone is not a perfect utopia, Sarah can be proud of her newfound assertiveness and children's books. Once she has achieved what she set out to do, she will look for a new goal to set for herself that she might have previously set aside.

Adam

An only child, Adam got a lot of attention from his parents as he was growing up. Now that he's an adult, though, his parents use him as a sounding board for their marital difficulties and constant negative comments about each other. For a long time, Adam felt guilty for not listening to them and not taking care of them, especially since they were always there for him while he was growing up. Adam's mental health was negatively affected, and his outlook on relationships was becoming bleak. He began to argue more with his wife and distance himself emotionally from her. His loyalty to his parents was strong and unwavering, but his wife insisted that he see a professional about his changes in mood and behavior.

Adam was in his Shit Zone with his parents, but he didn't want to 'betray' them and all that they had done for him by letting go of the value he had always placed on family cohesion. With time, though, Adam was able to recognize that he can still hold true to his value system without sacrificing himself and his health. After establishing more appropriate boundaries, Adam feels a sense of relief that he no longer needs to be the sounding board for either parent, because they have found a professional of their own with whom to talk. This has allowed him to view his parents as he did when he was younger, and he's no longer displacing the negativity that he was absorbing from them onto his wife.

Adam's Shit Zone has been shifted to a Happy Zone where he has set boundaries for himself without sacrificing his values regarding his parents. Adam has also learned to accept that what happens between his parents needs to be their responsibility, especially since he has now done everything he could for them. Therefore, his acceptance of the uncertainty of their prognosis has reduced his feelings of helplessness and constant worry.

Jasmine

Jasmine, a high school student, has always been a perfectionist. She worked hard at different aspects of her life—academics, sports, music—and had achieved more than most students in her grade. As life does, the older she got, however, the more complicated her studies became, which meant she had to work harder to achieve the same results. This contributed significantly to symptoms of anxiety, which persisted and spilled over into other aspects of Jasmine's life, including her social life. She feared being judged by others for not being smart or for being boring, and she feared letting down her teachers and parents. As she began to isolate herself from others and focus on her academic coursework, the only part of her identity she felt she could control – the academic, she neglected other areas of her life, which led to more anxiety and depressive symptoms.

Jasmine was in her Shit Zone. Her parents reached out for help, but Jasmine was resistant to change. People might think that meant that she was weak—or even worse, stupid. In reality, nothing could have been further from the truth. Jasmine resisted change and held tightly to her Shit Zone because it served a purpose for her. (This will be explored in the next chapters.) Nevertheless, with time, Jasmine has been able to move into a Happy Zone by realizing and accepting the fact that she cannot control what other people think of her, no matter what she does. Exploring other aspects of her identity has helped Jasmine see that she is much more than just a student, thus reducing her perfectionist drive. Accepting that she will never be perfect has also been a helpful factor in her Happy Zone.

As demonstrated in these examples, the Happy Zone can look different to each person, depending on what their Shit Zone looks like. One person's Happy Zone may be a Shit Zone for someone else, and vice versa. Therefore, the emphasis on the Happy Zone is not that a person is happy all the time, but that the person is doing whatever they can to realistically satisfy their values, desires, and health needs.

Any Holes in Your Cheese?

37

After reading this chapter, did you change your mind about what you wrote earlier? If so, use this space to write down the things you actually want in life.

CHAPTER 3

Research Behind Change

Before we discuss the process of shifting from the Shit Zone to the Happy Zone, we must first explain the empirical research that has looked into change and its processes. First, a definition: Among the many different meanings of *change*, the most relevant for our purposes, according to the Merriam-Webster dictionary is "to undergo transformation, transition, or substitution" and "to become different." Change is the process by which something or someone is altered in some way.

Becoming different or transforming does not mean that upon making the shift into a Happy Zone, you will become someone else; instead, you just become a different version of yourself. The changes to which we are referring are external behaviors that lead to more internal (emotional and psychological) peace. Of course, change does not occur in the same way with each person. Various practical factors influence if and how we change as individuals. These factors are purely explanatory and subjective, and do not apply to every person in every situation.

Age is one factor. (These are not in order of importance.) The younger you are, the less likely you are to avoid change. The older you are, though, the more likely it is that your changes will be well thought out rather than impulsive.

Personality is another factor. To discuss and quantify personality, though, we need to discuss temperament or disposition. Simply put, it is our behavioral tendencies based on our personality traits. For instance, people who are shy or fearful might not necessarily engage and see the world in a way that entices them to change easily, compared to people with more nonchalant and adaptable temperaments.

Personality

Personality traits have been found to influence our ability to accept and undergo change. If we explore Costa and McCrae's (1992) Big Five personality traits (E, N, C, A, O), we can see how some traits have been found to be more receptive to change. Extraversion (E), for instance, refers to the fact that a person can either feel drained during long periods of exposure to social situations (low extraversion, better known as introversion) or feel energized and rejuvenated by it (high extraversion, known as extraversion). Research indicates that people who score average or high on the extraversion scale are more likely to welcome change. This is not to say that introverts do not change, but that they are not keen to do so because of the risks that might be involved. However, when they do change, they often cope and accept change well when they plan for it properly.

Similarly, people who score average or high on openness to experience (O) and agreeableness (A) also tend to be less resistant to change. Openness to experience refers to a person's tendency to be imaginative, aesthetically sensitive, interested in new challenges and experiences, and intellectually curious. Someone who is open to experience is more likely to step out of their comfort zone, regardless of how they do so.

Agreeableness refers to a person's traits in terms of trust, straightforwardness, altruism, compliance, modesty, and sympathy. People who score average or high on agreeableness are usually willing to compromise for changes in their lives, since they tend to be more cooperative and willing to change. This isn't always a good thing, since they might compromise more than is necessary and sacrifice their own well-being to satisfy other people.

Neuroticism refers to emotional stability in the context of psychological stress. People who score high on neuroticism (N) react negatively to change and the stress that change can bring; they tend to adjust poorly to change and prefer routine.

Finally, conscientiousness refers to a person's tendency to be organized, dependable, self-disciplined, act dutifully, aim for achievement, and plan rather than act impulsively. People high in conscientiousness (C) do not actively seek out change and prefer things to be organized and structured. When they are presented with change, however, they'll take it on as a challenge and want to perfect it. Conversely, people low in conscientiousness prefer not to engage in change and will usually procrastinate or deny change altogether.

Another significant contributor to our acceptance of the process of change is our socialization. Parents, family, community beliefs, and behaviors are important in the way we are socialized to think about change in general. "This is how things are done" is an example of sustaining the status quo, regardless of our feelings about it. The thoughts, attitudes, and behaviors of our parents and significant others in our lives inform us of the ways we *should* feel and behave toward change and difficult endeavors. Fear of and aversion to change leads to limiting beliefs for people growing up in that kind of environment.

The final influencer to the process of change is our own cumulative life experiences. The more change a person experiences successfully in their life, the more likely they are to accept change as it comes. This does not mean that they will succeed at change or even like it, but it does suggest that they won't be as likely to resist it as other people might be. Acquiring the tools, skills, and wisdom that come with such experiences builds a sense of confidence and comfort with the idea of change. Of course, consistency in life is important, but just as depicted in the philosophy of yin and yang, consistency must also give way to change when it is necessary.

What about what helps with change? The two main encouragers of change are trust and empowerment, which go hand in hand. The Oxford dictionary defines *trust* as "the firm belief in the reliability, effectiveness, and ability of someone or something." One interesting thing about trust is that we *feel* it, rather than consciously think about it. We don't consciously think about *why* we trust someone or something until something bad happens to make us question that trust.

Consider a close friend, you might not consciously think about how or when you came to trust them, but if they betray you, you can consciously say that you've lost trust in them. When that happens, trust is transformed from a subconscious feeling to a conscious thought. The factor that changed in your relationship to your friend was your reliance on the consistency of their behavioral qualities and your perception of those qualities. The problem with that expectation is that people can never be 100 percent consistent, because we constantly change as we grow. The consequence of this unrealistic expectation of perfect consistency in others is that we lose trust in many people in different ways.

We have the same unrealistic expectation when it comes to trust and change. We assume that if we consider all the variables and factors of change, everything will go as planned and we will succeed and feel better. If only life was so linear! Unfortunately, we are not in control of most of the things we think we are. The only thing we can truly control is our behavior. Life is just too chaotic and complicated to follow the unrealistic equation that we set for it: A+B=C. It's too simplistic a thought for such a complex existence. So when our trust depends on factors outside ourselves, we lose that trust, avoid situations and people, and thus resist change. But if we trust in the only thing that we can realistically trust—ourselves—we can feel more confident that we will be fine, regardless of the outcome of change. If we struggle with trust in ourselves, then we need to get our trust on. "How?" you might ask. Be consistent in the way that you behave, and eventually you will learn to trust yourself again.

Let's talk about trust in relationships. When we decide to enter into a relationship, we develop a level—ideally a realistic level—of trust in the other person.

Most of the time, though, we simply trust people too much, which leads to disappointment and a sense of mistrust. For instance, we expect that our partner will *NEVER* lie to us or flirt with someone else, which is completely unrealistic. We all lie in one way or another in different ways on a daily basis. Also, engaging in harmless flirting is a natural tendency for many of us, since we like the sense of belonging and attention. The mistrust we might develop if we think that our partner is lying leads to anxious, accusatory, and hurtful behavior towards the partner that could result in the thing we originally feared: a breakup. However, if we have a more realistic mind-set about relationships and trust in ourselves to survive and get through the pain and emotional heartache that may come along, our fears and worries that lead to mistrust will subside.

There is a continuous psychological struggle that takes place when a person consciously decides to make a change in their life. That struggle is between the conscious desire to change and the unconscious fears about losing their comfort zone and sense of identity. (The identity part will be discussed in the next chapter.) Research on the process of change has given rise to various models and stages that help explain what happens to a person during the process of change. Let's explore a couple of them.

Satir's Model of Change

This model was devised by family therapist Virginia Satir in the 1990s. It is widely used for organizational change, but it has been adapted as a way to understand individual change as well. The Satir model includes different stages of adjustment. The first stage is the last status quo: the person's life is in a state of routine and comfort. This might be frustrating (or not) to the person, but it is a place that is familiar and constant.

A shift to stage two requires a foreign element, an event that shakes the stability and familiarity of how things are and causes a rift in the routine. The event does not have to be an actual event; it could also be a thought that's foreign to the person. At this time, the person may either resist its existence and deny it altogether, using blocking tactics, or open themselves up to the foreign event and become aware of its purpose.

Enter stage three: chaos. Here, the event puts the person in a place with which they are unfamiliar. Feelings of anxiety, distress, discomfort, and so on arise during this stage, since the person needs to now become a bit more creative and figure out how to get themselves back to the status quo. They will come up with a multitude of different ideas to help them shift into the fourth stage: practice and integration.

Here, new ideas and behaviors are put into action. People explore what does and doesn't work for them as they make mistakes, which is inevitable, but eventually they'll learn from those mistakes. Finally, we walk into the new status quo where behaviors start to level off. As things become less chaotic and uncertain, people develop more confidence, trust, and knowledge in the formation of the new status quo.

Transtheoretical Model of Change

This model was formulated by James O. Prochaska and Carlo DiClemente in 1977. It is integrative and conceptualizes the process of change. The transtheoretical model of change involves five stages and, at times, a sixth extension.

The first stage is the pre-contemplation stage (yep, it's in the name), where change has not yet been seriously considered. A person might not necessarily see anything problematic in their behavior and engage in various defenses to avoid that awareness. Examples of that include feeling reluctance or resistance to change, rebelling against doing so, resigned to defeat, and making excuses or rationalizing themselves out of a necessary change. The second stage is the contemplation stage, during which a shift happens and the person begins to recognize that a problem exists. This recognition allows the person to start considering the possibility of change.

During preparation, the third stage, a mental and physical preparation begins to ensure that change can occur. The person begins to take baby steps to move themselves into stage four, which is where the plan is put into action and behavioral changes are made. Finally, in the maintenance stage, which is a continuous stage, the person avoids relapsing into old behaviors. The sixth extension, termination, was added as a way to recognize that sometimes old behaviors might be repeated. That should not end the cycle, but it must be acknowledged and weighed in with certain behavioral changes such as smoking, drinking, and substance addictions.

Who Do You *Think* You Are?

Here is a research-based personality test (not the fake-ass ones that you find on social media) that can help you understand a little more about yourself and how you respond to change. You can find and take it online. The International Personality Item Pool (IPIP) can be taken in the long form (300 items) or the short form (120 items) (Goldberg et al., 2006). This is a personality questionnaire that assesses people on the Big Five model of personality traits (Costa & McCrae, 1987) mentioned in the previous chapter.

So before you take it, write down where you think you score on the continuums of extroversion, conscientiousness, openness to experience, agreeableness, and neuroticism (low, average, high). Which model of change do you think would work best for you?

Stuck in Your Shit?

53

What do you think stops you from moving out of your Shit Zone? What is holding you back? What feelings come up when you consider leaving it—or even when you consider what life would be like out of it? Write down the feelings that come up for you and what worries you about the process of shifting.

CHAPTER 4

The Path from the SZ to the HZ

In order to properly describe the intricacies of shifting from a Shit Zone to a Happy Zone, visualization might be helpful:

This might look simple, but as you read this chapter, you'll see that it's not. Obviously, when making this change, various emotions arise. Those appearing in this diagram are not the only emotions that come up, but they are often the most important. Let's start with fear, since it is the most obvious.

Fear

There is an inherent fear associated with not knowing what will happen or what your destination might look like. Emotional well-being is not as concretely described as some other things in life, so it cannot be quantified and aimed for in the same way, which creates a fear of the unknown. The fourteenth-century saying "Better the devil you know than the devil you don't" usually reigns strong here.

Fear of not being happy once out of your Shit Zone also occurs: "I'm scared to put in all this effort for nothing." The fear of doing so much yet not achieving what you think is on the other side. This fear of failure leads you to think, *I don't want to try so hard and then have nothing change*. The fear of failure is probably one of the toughest ones to work through, since it is associated with perfectionism and unrealistic expectations.

When clients discuss failure, they describe a scenario where no matter what they do, they lose. Imagine wanting to get an A on your final exams or hoping to earn your first million by the age of thirty. Most people don't consider the many variables that might affect the likelihood of achieving such a narrow result.

Let's use the final exam as an example. You bust your ass to reread every chapter and review every lecture presentation and all your notes. You stress, hardly sleep or eat, and do nothing but study until the dreaded exam. You go back over every piece of information with a fine-tooth comb and memorize everything … But when you sit down to take the exam, you see that 50 percent of your grade will be based on a totally insignificant question that comes straight out of left field. Guess who's fucked? You panic and fail the exam—not because you haven't studied, but because your instructor hasn't gotten laid enough times and has sadistically opted to torture the class. So now you feel like a failure, and that slams your self-esteem and confidence, which snowballs into more negative thoughts and brings about destructive behaviors. You had believed that you could control your results if you just studied to the nth degree, but you missed out on so many external variables that are equally important to your success, such as your teacher, whoever created the exam, your mood, your studying—in other words, life!

The problem with feeling that you can control *anything* and *everything* other than your own behavior is that it creates the illusion that if you don't succeed, you have failed—and by extension, that *you* are a failure. The problem with this mind-set is that you give yourself a 1 percent success rate and you end up feeling like your failure rate is 99 percent. To not consider yourself a failure, the achievement must look exactly like this {x} and anything else is not good enough. Don't misunderstand! The fact that you cannot control everything shouldn't be used as an excuse for not trying and just giving in. On the contrary, when you accept that you are not in control of anything other than your own behavior, that should motivate you to do all that you can to achieve your goals—but also to peacefully accept things if you don't.

Wouldn't it be great if life was as nice and neat as what we want it to look like? Unfortunately life isn't so straightforward, and we don't exist in a vacuum where we can dictate how our lives move along. Working hard is important, but coming to terms with the fact that life is messy, and that we won't necessarily get what we want, helps us accept change more effectively and with less worry.

Worry

Although worry and fear are connected in many ways, the main difference is that worry is constant, a bit more subtle, and riddled with what-ifs. What if I'm still not happy? What if it takes too long? What if it's too late to change now? What if nothing I do works? What if no one accepts me after I change? What if I lose myself? What if I don't succeed? As you can see, these what-ifs are filled with negative and limiting thoughts that can discourage any motivation to change.

These types of statements make it hard to see the rewards in the Happy Zone and instead put a spotlight on the catastrophic possibilities that increase your resistance to change. Worrying about change blocks you from focusing on the baby steps that can get you to your Happy Zone. It also limits your ability to see the other possibilities in the path of change: the possibilities that you can get there, be happy, and stay there (if you do the work).

It's natural to worry about change, which can break up your routine and involve unknown variables. What's interesting about worry, however, is that most of what we worry about never actually happens. Yet, we devote lots of time and energy worrying about worst-case scenarios as a way to protect ourselves from getting hurt or failing. Some people worry about the fact that when they finally arrive at their Happy

Zone, they won't have anything else to look forward to or fight for. Sometimes, we self-sabotage so that we'll always have a goal to work toward, although this is usually a subconscious thought pattern.

Conversely, some folks worry about arriving at their Happy Zone but then falling back out of it, perhaps slipping all the way back to their Shit Zone or just out of the Happy Zone —sort of a one-step-forward, two-steps-back concept. Well, that particular worry is pointless, since slipping back is guaranteed to happen. You will step back every once in a while but if you keep pushing forward, you'll get out of your Shit Zone again—and this time a lot more quickly, because you've done it before. Change is continuous and must be worked on consistently to ensure its progress. It is not enough to get to your Happy Zone and then stop doing what you did to get there: you have to keep at it.

Imagine a person who is unhealthy, doesn't eat well, and lives a sedentary lifestyle. Tired of that Shit Zone, they decide to change and move toward a healthier lifestyle—their Happy Zone. They get rid of fast food, preservatives, unhealthy drinks, and start exercising. However, every once in a while they succumb to the temptation to go back to their old ways, which is fine and completely natural. The unrealistic expectation that everyone can change without taking a few steps back here and there is ridiculous and not conducive to change. That thought pattern just makes it more nerve-racking to consider changing and increases the worry of whether it's worth the effort to do so.

Guilt/Regret

Guilt and regret are probably two of the most difficult emotions for people to experience. But they are powerful elements of the change process because they're usually experienced as someone gets closer to their Happy Zone and even as they enter it. The Cambridge English dictionary defines *guilt* as a "feeling of worry or unhappiness that you have because you have done something wrong." Guilt usually results from doing something bad to someone else, but in this change process, it involves acting negatively to oneself. People typically feel guilty that they have allowed themselves to suffer in their Shit Zone for as long as they did. They feel guilty for not having cared about themselves enough, which then transforms into regret.

The Cambridge English dictionary defines *regret* as a "feeling of sadness about something sad or wrong, about a mistake that you have made, and a wish that it could have been different and better." Basically, to regret is to wish that something could have been done better. In the shift from the Shit Zone to the Happy Zone, people regret that they allowed themselves to stay in their Shit Zone and didn't act sooner. Hindsight is always 20/20; it's easy to fall into the regret trap when you're in your Happy Zone and realize that the shift was not as bad as you had expected. "If I had known then what I know now, I would've done this sooner." Well, you didn't know. Move on and stop wasting time and energy wallowing in what could have been. Move on to the here and now.

The biggest problem with hindsight is that it makes you judgmental and remarkably omniscient. You begin to tear yourself apart about what you could or should have done. Well, if you had known then what you know now, you would've done things differently, so give yourself a break. Stop being so judgy and get down off your high horse of knowledge. Regret and guilt force you to focus on the past rather than on the process of moving forward and finding more paths to where you want to be. Keeping your head in the past makes you more susceptible to staying put in your current Shit Zone—or even worse, taking this negative mind-set to your Happy Zone, which can then turn it into another Shit Zone. Lather, rinse, and repeat, anyone?

Sadness

Sadness is by far the most complicated and complex part of the path from the Shit Zone to the Happy Zone. Of course, regret, guilt, worry, and fear can all contribute to feelings of sadness. More than that, though, you feel a deep sadness for yourself because you're in this Shit Zone. Even if you think you deserve the bad things that are happening to you, you still feel sad for yourself, no matter how deeply you hide it behind self-deprecation. Sadness also comes with the realization that you might not necessarily know how to get out of your Shit Zone. Not knowing your path can make you feel sad for yourself, which is different from self-pity. You feel more like "I wish I had some direction in my life, and I'm not sure how to change this."

What do you do to minimize all the other emotions that stop you from trying to maneuver down this path while avoiding resistance? Asking for help is not always easy; it comes with a feeling of incompetence, which is usually a hit to your ego. For some people, seeking help makes them feel weak and not smart enough, but not asking for help leads to far worse degradation than asking for help ever does. Not asking keeps you in your Shit Zone longer, which contributes to lower self-esteem, self-worth, and self-confidence, and impacts other essential aspects of your identity.

Sadness also arises from the grieving that a person goes through when shifting to the Happy Zone. Think of it this way: the person you are in the Shit Zone has to change in some ways in order to successfully shift into the Happy Zone. Basically you have to say "Goodbye" to Shit-Zone you and "Hello" to Happy-Zone you. Grieving Shit-Zone you involves a certain level of sadness, which might seem like a ridiculous concept considering that moving on to Happy-Zone you is the goal. So why the hell would you be sad that Shit-Zone you is gone—or at the very least, minimized in significance?

Well, the reality is that Shit-Zone you *was* functional in some ways. Being in your Shit Zone served a purpose. You may not know what the purpose or functionality of it was, and letting go of that person is part of the grieving process that helps you move on. You stayed in your Shit Zone because it helped you cope with something in your life, so losing that *functional* version of yourself can be scary and sad. The reason why functional is in quotations is because even though Shit-Zone you serves a function, it is actually *dysfunctional* in nature, or else you wouldn't be in a Shit Zone.

Here's an example. Now thirty-one years old, Mika has been suffering with anxiety for many years. She started work on a master's degree in business administration a year ago, and now she's having difficulty controlling her worries about her grades and her health. She constantly feels inadequate, puts more pressure on herself than anybody could handle, and berates herself when she doesn't perform well. She has ignored her anxiety for many years, and now she has developed physiological symptoms—heart racing, difficulty breathing, fatigue, sweats, nausea, and dizziness—that last throughout the day. Mika's family and friends have urged her to see a therapist or at least talk to a doctor regarding her anxiety. However, she consistently refuses to admit that she suffers with anxiety, choosing instead to chalk her problems up to stress. As time passes, Mika's anxiety is worsening. She has now suffered a panic attack and developed gastrointestinal difficulties, but she still refuses to get help.

This is an example of Shit-Zone Mika. Shit-Zone Mika seems functional to herself in many ways. Coming from a traditional background, she has convinced herself that she doesn't have anxiety or mental health difficulties, and she doesn't want to associate herself with anyone she considers to be weak. (Although we know that people suffering with mental health difficulties are definitely *not* weak). However, to Mika having anxiety would mean that she can't handle her life properly. So Shit-Zone Mika's main function is to make Mika feel like she's in control of her life. Being in her Shit Zone makes Mika feel better about herself, even though the truth is that Shit-Zone Mika is actually dysfunctional and will hurt Mika even more in the long run.

Let's conceptualize this chapter using the example of a previous client of mine. Rayyan

Rayyan was the eldest of two boys in his family. His father and mother are still married but had their fair share of arguments while he was growing up, and he witnessed his mother back down from every argument until his father's death five years ago. Rayyan maintains a strong relationship with his mother, but he suffered the loss of his brother to cancer and has been struggling with depressive symptoms ever since.

Now twenty-four years old, Rayyan has been dating his girlfriend for a year and a half. However, she is a dominating, controlling woman who constantly criticizes everything he does, and he has been unhappy in the relationship for the past eight months. Rayyan wants to end their relationship so that he can find someone more suited to his emotional needs, but he hasn't been able to express that to his girlfriend. Rayyan is in his Shit Zone.

Through therapy, Rayyan becomes aware of his fear of retaliation from his girlfriend if he tries to leave the relationship. He is scared that his girlfriend, who gets along well with his mother, will get his mom to side with her, and then he'll have to fight both of them. He's also afraid that he'll fail if he tries to end the relationship, which would then give his girlfriend "ammunition" to hold against him. She would always be able to say to him, "You tried to leave me," and use that as a form of emotional manipulation to keep him around.

These fears lead to many 'what if' scenarios in Rayyan's mind, like: *What if I end up alone? What if nobody ever loves me again? What if I can't find better? What if I can't ever get out of this relationship?* Nevertheless, Rayyan starts the process of moving out of his Shit Zone into his Happy Zone. But as he gets close, he starts to feel guilt and regret that he didn't make a shift sooner and that he fluctuated in and out of the relationship because he was weak. He also experiences feelings of sadness because he has nobody except his therapist to talk with about getting out of the relationship. He feels sad that Shit-Zone Rayyan has had to suffer for so long, which leads to additional feelings of guilt and regret.

From Rayyan's example, you can see that this process is neither simple nor straightforward. Every time he takes a few steps forward, he then takes a few backward. Through persistence and determination, however, Rayyan is eventually able to progress through his Shit Zone and onto a more forward path to his Happy Zone.

Now that we've conceptualized what the path might involve, it's also important to discuss the overriding feeling that will always preside over the process of change. That feeling is overwhelming intensity. Try to imagine being in a Shit Zone and wanting to get out of it—everything around you is too much, and it feels as if nothing you could ever do would make enough of a change for it to matter. You would find so many things that need changing, and it would feel so overwhelming that it would be easier to stay in your Shit Zone. However, staying in that zone only adds more variables, and in doing so you are delaying the inevitable and adding more variables to something that is already complicated.

There is no reason to assume that the shift and change from Shit Zone to Happy Zone won't be difficult or painful. Even though things might cognitively seem common-sensical and *duh*-worthy, this change is associated with feelings that can be powerful and even crippling. Simply put, stop being so hard on yourself when you're going through change.

Light-Bulb Moment, Anyone?

Did any of those feelings strike a chord for you? What awareness did you gain from reading that chapter? Obviously, as you become more aware of the things that stop you from moving forward, you're one step further than where you were when you first started reading. Write down everything that came up for you as you were reading this chapter. If you identify, then clarify. Be specific about what came up and how it has stopped you. Be clear about why you have allowed these emotions to get in the way of your progress.

Get to Your Happy Zone! Questions to Get You on Your Way

Remember how I said that this is not a self-help book? Well, I wasn't lying. I don't have any magical advice that's going to help everyone move into their Happy Zone. However, I've tried to give you insight and increase your awareness into what happens in change and why we resist it. With this knowledge, you will need to find the right formula that works for you in how to move from any Shit Zone which you find yourself in to a Happy Zone. Even though I am not going to throw out any advice about how to make that shift, I can give you some tips and questions to help you figure out how to avoid resisting change:

1. Find the function of your current Shit Zone. What purpose does it serve?

2. What does your Happy Zone look like? *Don't say, "I feel happy in it."* Be concrete. "I'll go to the gym three times a week, lose five pounds, let go of my toxic relationship, or reach out to my parents on a daily basis." Be specific and quantifiable. Use the SMART philosophy by George Doran

and colleagues when conceptualizing your Happy Zone. Specific. Measurable. Achievable. Realistic. Time-based. This is where most people are unsuccessful. Their concept of happy is too abstract and idealistic, which makes it almost impossible to achieve. Don't make that mistake.

3. Whatever feelings come up during the process, write them down and deal with them at a later time. *Do not* stop yourself from doing what needs to be done just because you feel something holding you back. You should make time to explore those feelings, process them, and work through them, but only after you have dealt with your shit.

4. Highlight your achievements and don't focus on your drawbacks. Essentially this means don't beat yourself up every time you get something wrong. Just figure out what went wrong and how to get past it. But make sure to always recognize your achievements, no matter how small and insignificant you think they are.

5. Look for what motivates you. Basically, give yourself a big enough reason for why you are making the change. Make it important enough and make it matter, because if it doesn't matter,

fighting through your shit will be much tougher. If you can't find a really good reason, just remember that you look like shit in your Shit Zone.

6. If you like to celebrate your achievements, make sure that shit is like the Fourth of fucking July. If you like patting yourself on the back, make sure you leave a handprint. If you need a carrot at the end of the stick, then tie one on. Use any tools you can to keep yourself going.

7. If you fail, get your ass up and do it again. Don't make excuses, and don't give yourself an out. People don't usually regret the things at which they fail; they regret not trying.

This isn't a self-help book. It's a wake-up call. So get out of bed!

Gun to Your Head. Pen to Paper

Answer the seven questions listed above. Do it, now! You know that if you don't do it now, you'll set this book aside and forget why the hell you picked it up to begin with. No excuses, no bullshit, no lame-ass "I don't have time, I'll do it later." Get your shit together and get out of it.

Back to the Beginning

Let's bring this full circle now. Remember the three things you mentioned at the beginning of this book? Let's revisit them. Since reading this book, have any of those things conceptually changed in any way?

If they didn't change, that's great. Get on with it then. There's no reason for you to be in a place where you are not working to achieve them.

If they did change, then use this page to detail the steps you are going to take to achieve them. Also make notes to remind yourself about what stopped you from taking these steps previously, so that you won't do that again.

High fucking five, you have now exited your shit.

81

REFERENCES

Andreas, Steve., & Satir, V 1991. *Virginia Satir: The Patterns of Her Magic.* Palo Alto, CA: Science and Behavior Books.

DiClemente, Carlo C., and James O. Prochaska. 1977. "Toward a Comprehensive, Transtheoretical Model of Change: Stages of Change and Addictive Behaviors." In *Applied Clinical Psychology: Treating Addictive Behaviors*, 2nd. ed., edited by William R. Miller and Nick Heather, 3–24. New York: Plenum.

Doran, George T. 1981. "There's a S.M.A.R.T. Way to Write Management's Goals and Objectives." *Management Review* 70, no. 11: 35–36.

Freud, Anna. 1937. *The Ego and the Mechanisms of Defence.* Translated by Cecil Baines. London: Hogarth.

Goldberg, Lewis R., and John Johnson, Herbert W. Eber, Robert Hogan, Michael C. Ashton, Robert Cloninger, et al. 2006. "The International Personality Item Pool and the Future of

Public-Domain Personality Measures." *Journal of Research in Personality* 40: 84–96.

McCrae, Robert R., and Paul T. Costa. 1987. "Validation of the Five-Factor Model of Personality Across Instruments and Observers." *Journal of Personality and Social Psychology* 52, no. 1: 81–90.

ABOUT THE AUTHOR

Dr. Thoraiya Kanafani is a PhD graduate in the department of clinical psychology from Walden University in the United States. Before that, she completed a bachelor's degree in psychology and master's degrees in educational psychology and another in counseling psychology in Canada. After completing her education in Canada and working in many different settings, she moved to the Middle East and has worked in countries such as Bahrain, Lebanon, and Saudi Arabia. She is a Canadian and United Arab Emirates licensed psychologist. She has been featured in magazines and newspapers, and has presented on various topics in psychology on radio and TV shows. She is a regular guest speaker on the Dubai Eye radio station. Dr. Kanafani has conducted many workshops and presented seminars on various topics pertaining to psychology and mental health. She has close to fifteen years of experience in the field of psychology and mental health. She moved to Dubai in 2013 to work as a clinical psychologist and director at the Human Relations Institute and Clinics, which she took over with her colleague Sabine Skaf. She is also a part-time lecturer at Middlesex University and Heriot-Watt University, where she teaches undergraduate and graduate psychology courses.

www.ingramcontent.com/pod-product-compliance
Lightning Source LLC
Chambersburg PA
CBHW031135250726

48655CB00002B/680